# THE ESSENTIAL ESSENTIAL BOOK OF KAKURO

D1399589

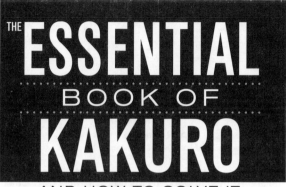

# THE ESSENTIAL BOOK OF KAKURO

## AND HOW TO SOLVE IT

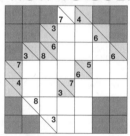

GARETH MOORE

**ATRIA** BOOKS

New York  London  Toronto  Sydney

**ATRIA** BOOKS
1230 Avenue of the Americas
New York, NY 10020

ISBN-13: 978-0-7432-9441-6
ISBN-10:    0-7432-9441-6

First Atria Books trade paperback edition December 2005

1  3  5  7  9  10  8  6  4  2

**ATRIA** BOOKS is a trademark of Simon & Schuster, Inc.

Manufactured in the United States of America

For information about special discounts for bulk purchases,
please contact Simon & Schuster Special Sales at
1-800-456-6798 or business@simonandschuster.com.

# INTRODUCTION

Kakuro, the name of which derives from a contraction of the Japanese word for "addition" and the Japanese pronunciation of the English word "cross," is a puzzle and logic game that's simple to learn and yet challenging to master. It can perhaps be thought of as a crossword puzzle featuring numbers rather than letters.

But there's more to Kakuro than this. It can also be compared to Su Doku, the number-placing puzzle craze, because repeating a digit is forbidden within a clue area, and the only valid digits are the numbers 1 to 9.

And, just like Su Doku, you don't need to be a mathematical genius to solve Kakuro puzzles. In fact, you don't need to do any maths at all, because we've included a list of all the sums you'll ever need to play every puzzle in this book. What are you waiting for?

# HOW TO PLAY

The grids vary in size but they all work the same way. Each puzzle is made up of a combination of solid and "clue" squares, as well as empty squares grouped into discrete units, each called a "run," the aim being to fill each empty square with a single digit from 1 to 9. Zero is never a valid digit, and within each run a figure must not appear twice.

Unlike crosswords, the clues of a Kakuro puzzle are contained inside each grid, so you don't need to keep looking away as you solve the puzzle. Each horizontal and vertical "run" of empty squares starts with a shaded "clue" square, positioned immediately to its left (for horizontal runs), or above (for vertical runs); a run ends when stopped by a solid square or another clue square. A clue square is split in two by a diagonal line, and will contain either one or two numbers, each called a "clue." The clue positioned above the diagonal line gives the total that all the digits in that horizontal run must add up to; similarly, the clue number below the diagonal line in a clue square positioned above a vertical run gives the sum that the empty squares *below* that clue must equal.

What gives the puzzles their fun and fascinating twist is that no digit can be repeated within a single vertical or horizontal run. So, for example, a 4 cannot be formed from the digits 2 and 2, but can only be made from 1 and 3. This means that logical reasoning is required to establish which digits will fit where.

## SOLVING A PUZZLE

It doesn't take very long before combinations of clues can be spotted that allow the solving of the puzzle to begin. For example, in the grid below, note that in the bottom-left empty square the clues 4 (down) and 3 (across) overlap in the box here labeled "a":

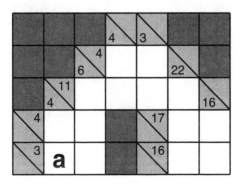

It's clear that 1 and 2 is a valid combination to make 3, and that 1 and 3 is a valid combination for making 4. This means that box "a" must contain one of 1, 2 or 3. But if it contained 3 then there would be no valid combination for the clue "3" since 0 cannot be used, and if it contained 2 then there would be no valid combination for the clue "4" since we cannot use the same digit twice (that is 2 and 2). Therefore, it can only be 1.

Following this reasoning, if "a" is 1 then the cell above must contain 3 (since 1 + 3 equals 4) and similarly the cell on its right must contain 2. This can also be applied to the two cells above. The illustration below demonstrates these steps:

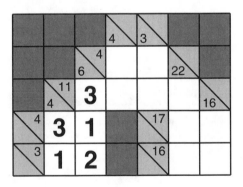

Now, the same reasoning about valid totals for 3 and 4 can be applied to solve the top section of the puzzle:

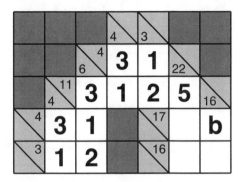

And, finally, the bottom-right part can be solved in a similar way. Notice that 16 can only be made up of 7 and 9, since 8 and 8 would repeat the same digit, while other combinations such as 6 and 10 are invalid because only numbers 1 to 9 can be used. Similarly, 17 must be made up of 8 and 9. The only common digit in this case is 9, so the cell, above labeled "b," must be 9.

Solving the remainder of the puzzle can be achieved using simple mathematics:

And that's all there is to it!

# ADVANCED SOLVING TIPS

Thinking about valid digit combinations is all that is required to solve the puzzles in this book, but there are some tricks that will help too. And, while it may sound obvious, use a pencil to mark in the possible combinations of numbers for each empty square, which can then be eliminated as you go along.

## ADDING UP AREAS

Knowing that the total of the digits in the grid as a whole (excluding the clues) is always the same whether you add them up horizontally or vertically can help to solve small areas of the puzzle. For example, in the grid above, the horizontal clues at bottom left are 4 and 3, which total 7. The clues running down into this bottom-left area are 4 and 6, totalling 10. The difference between the sum of the vertical and horizontal clues (10 − 7) is 3, and 3 will be the value of the cell that is in one area but not the other. This is indeed the case, and can be seen above in the hatched square.

## ELIMINATING DIGIT PAIRS

If you have worked out that a run consists of, for example, only a 1 or a 3 in one square and only a 1 or a 3 in another square, then it follows that there *cannot* be a 1 or a 3 anywhere else in the run, since between the two cells both digits are already accounted for.

# THE PUZZLES IN THIS BOOK

You should never need to guess when solving the puzzles in this book—*all* of them can be solved by thinking about the possible orders of digits within each run and making certain eliminations based on this. On the other hand, when you have only got a couple of options for a square sometimes guessing works very well—but it's never compulsory!

There are five difficulty levels: Easy (Level 1), Moderate (Level 2), Difficult (Level 3), Very Hard (Level 4) and Extreme (Level 5). The Easy puzzles require simpler logic-solving than the later puzzles, so they're a good place to get the hang of things. The Extreme puzzles are for when you have truly mastered the art of Kakuro! If you can solve them without guessing then you are doing very well.

Each puzzle has a unique solution, which is given at the back of the book.

# VALID DIGIT COMBINATIONS

These lists of valid number combinations for a given clue total, and for clue lengths of 2, 3, 4, 5 and 6 squares, are useful for working out which digits may work in certain runs.

# CLUES OF LENGTH 2:

| To make: | Combinations: |
|---|---|
| 3: | 1,2; |
| 4: | 1,3; |
| 5: | 1,4; 2,3; |
| 6: | 1,5; 2,4; |
| 7: | 1,6; 2,5; 3,4; |
| 8: | 1,7; 2,6; 3,5; |
| 9: | 1,8; 2,7; 3,6; 4,5; |
| 10: | 1,9; 2,8; 3,7; 4,6; |
| 11: | 2,9; 3,8; 4,7; 5,6; |
| 12: | 3,9; 4,8; 5,7; |
| 13: | 4,9; 5,8; 6,7; |
| 14: | 5,9; 6,8; |
| 15: | 6,9; 7,8; |
| 16: | 7,9; |
| 17: | 8,9; |

# CLUES OF LENGTH 3:

| | |
|---|---|
| 6: | 1,2,3; |
| 7: | 1,2,4; |
| 8: | 1,2,5; 1,3,4; |
| 9: | 1,2,6; 1,3,5; 2,3,4; |
| 10: | 1,2,7; 1,3,6; 1,4,5; 2,3,5; |
| 11: | 1,2,8; 1,3,7; 1,4,6; 2,3,6; 2,4,5; |
| 12: | 1,2,9; 1,3,8; 1,4,7; 1,5,6; 2,3,7; 2,4,6; 3,4,5; |
| 13: | 1,3,9; 1,4,8; 1,5,7; 2,3,8; 2,4,7; 2,5,6; 3,4,6; |
| 14: | 1,4,9; 1,5,8; 1,6,7; 2,3,9; 2,4,8; 2,5,7; 3,4,7; 3,5,6; |
| 15: | 1,5,9; 1,6,8; 2,4,9; 2,5,8; 2,6,7; 3,4,8; 3,5,7; 4,5,6; |
| 16: | 1,6,9; 1,7,8; 2,5,9; 2,6,8; 3,4,9; 3,5,8; 3,6,7; 4,5,7; |
| 17: | 1,7,9; 2,6,9; 2,7,8; 3,5,9; 3,6,8; 4,5,8; 4,6,7; |
| 18: | 1,8,9; 2,7,9; 3,6,9; 3,7,8; 4,5,9; 4,6,8; 5,6,7; |
| 19: | 2,8,9; 3,7,9; 4,6,9; 4,7,8; 5,6,8; |
| 20: | 3,8,9; 4,7,9; 5,6,9; 5,7,8; |
| 21: | 4,8,9; 5,7,9; 6,7,8; |
| 22: | 5,8,9; 6,7,9; |
| 23: | 6,8,9; |
| 24: | 7,8,9; |

# CLUES OF LENGTH 4:

10: 1,2,3,4;

11: 1,2,3,5;

12: 1,2,3,6; 1,2,4,5;

13: 1,2,3,7; 1,2,4,6; 1,3,4,5;

14: 1,2,3,8; 1,2,4,7; 1,2,5,6; 1,3,4,6; 2,3,4,5;

15: 1,2,3,9; 1,2,4,8; 1,2,5,7; 1,3,4,7; 1,3,5,6; 2,3,4,6;

16: 1,2,4,9; 1,2,5,8; 1,3,4,8; 1,3,5,7; 1,4,5,6; 2,3,4,7; 2,3,5,6;

17: 1,2,5,9; 1,2,6,8; 1,3,4,9; 1,3,5,8; 1,3,6,7; 1,4,5,7; 2,3,4,8; 2,3,5,7; 2,4,5,6;

18: 1,2,6,9; 1,2,7,8; 1,3,5,9; 1,3,6,8; 1,4,5,8; 1,4,6,7; 2,3,4,9; 2,3,5,8; 2,3,6,7; 2,4,5,7; 3,4,5,6;

19: 1,2,7,9; 1,3,6,9; 1,3,7,8; 1,4,5,9; 1,4,6,8; 1,5,6,7; 2,3,5,9; 2,3,6,8; 2,4,5,8; 2,4,6,7; 3,4,5,7;

20: 1,2,8,9; 1,3,7,9; 1,4,6,9; 1,4,7,8; 1,5,6,8; 2,3,6,9; 2,3,7,8; 2,4,5,9; 2,4,6,8; 2,5,6,7; 3,4,5,8; 3,4,6,7;

21: 1,3,8,9; 1,4,7,9; 1,5,6,9; 1,5,7,8; 2,3,7,9; 2,4,6,9; 2,4,7,8; 2,5,6,8; 3,4,5,9; 3,4,6,8; 3,5,6,7;

22: 1,4,8,9; 1,5,7,9; 1,6,7,8; 2,3,8,9; 2,4,7,9; 2,5,6,9; 2,5,7,8; 3,4,6,9; 3,4,7,8; 3,5,6,8; 4,5,6,7;

23: 1,5,8,9; 1,6,7,9; 2,4,8,9; 2,5,7,9; 2,6,7,8; 3,4,7,9; 3,5,6,9; 3,5,7,8; 4,5,6,8;

24: 1,6,8,9; 2,5,8,9; 2,6,7,9; 3,4,8,9; 3,5,7,9; 3,6,7,8; 4,5,6,9; 4,5,7,8;

25: 1,7,8,9; 2,6,8,9; 3,5,8,9; 3,6,7,9; 4,5,7,9; 4,6,7,8;

26: 2,7,8,9; 3,6,8,9; 4,5,8,9; 4,6,7,9; 5,6,7,8;

27: 3,7,8,9; 4,6,8,9; 5,6,7,9;

28: 4,7,8,9; 5,6,8,9;

29: 5,7,8,9;

30: 6,7,8,9;

# CLUES OF LENGTH 5:

15: 1,2,3,4,5;
16: 1,2,3,4,6;
17: 1,2,3,4,7; 1,2,3,5,6;
18: 1,2,3,4,8; 1,2,3,5,7; 1,2,4,5,6;
19: 1,2,3,4,9; 1,2,3,5,8; 1,2,3,6,7; 1,2,4,5,7; 1,3,4,5,6;
20: 1,2,3,5,9; 1,2,3,6,8; 1,2,4,5,8; 1,2,4,6,7; 1,3,4,5,7; 2,3,4,5,6;
21: 1,2,3,6,9; 1,2,3,7,8; 1,2,4,5,9; 1,2,4,6,8; 1,2,5,6,7; 1,3,4,5,8; 1,3,4,6,7; 2,3,4,5,7;
22: 1,2,3,7,9; 1,2,4,6,9; 1,2,4,7,8; 1,2,5,6,8; 1,3,4,5,9; 1,3,4,6,8; 1,3,5,6,7; 2,3,4,5,8; 2,3,4,6,7;
23: 1,2,3,8,9; 1,2,4,7,9; 1,2,5,6,9; 1,2,5,7,8; 1,3,4,6,9; 1,3,4,7,8; 1,3,5,6,8; 1,4,5,6,7; 2,3,4,5,9; 2,3,4,6,8; 2,3,5,6,7;
24: 1,2,4,8,9; 1,2,5,7,9; 1,2,6,7,8; 1,3,4,7,9; 1,3,5,6,9; 1,3,5,7,8; 1,4,5,6,8; 2,3,4,6,9; 2,3,4,7,8; 2,3,5,6,8; 2,4,5,6,7;
25: 1,2,5,8,9; 1,2,6,7,9; 1,3,4,8,9; 1,3,5,7,9; 1,3,6,7,8; 1,4,5,6,9; 1,4,5,7,8; 2,3,4,7,9; 2,3,5,6,9; 2,3,5,7,8; 2,4,5,6,8; 3,4,5,6,7;
26: 1,2,6,8,9; 1,3,5,8,9; 1,3,6,7,9; 1,4,5,7,9; 1,4,6,7,8; 2,3,4,8,9; 2,3,5,7,9; 2,3,6,7,8; 2,4,5,6,9; 2,4,5,7,8; 3,4,5,6,8;
27: 1,2,7,8,9; 1,3,6,8,9; 1,4,5,8,9; 1,4,6,7,9; 1,5,6,7,8; 2,3,5,8,9; 2,3,6,7,9; 2,4,5,7,9; 2,4,6,7,8; 3,4,5,6,9; 3,4,5,7,8;
28: 1,3,7,8,9; 1,4,6,8,9; 1,5,6,7,9; 2,3,6,8,9; 2,4,5,8,9; 2,4,6,7,9; 2,5,6,7,8; 3,4,5,7,9; 3,4,6,7,8;
29: 1,4,7,8,9; 1,5,6,8,9; 2,3,7,8,9; 2,4,6,8,9; 2,5,6,7,9; 3,4,5,8,9; 3,4,6,7,9; 3,5,6,7,8;
30: 1,5,7,8,9; 2,4,7,8,9; 2,5,6,8,9; 3,4,6,8,9; 3,5,6,7,9; 4,5,6,7,8;
31: 1,6,7,8,9; 2,5,7,8,9; 3,4,7,8,9; 3,5,6,8,9; 4,5,6,7,9;
32: 2,6,7,8,9; 3,5,7,8,9; 4,5,6,8,9;
33: 3,6,7,8,9; 4,5,7,8,9;
34: 4,6,7,8,9;
35: 5,6,7,8,9;

# CLUES OF LENGTH 6:

21: 1,2,3,4,5,6;
22: 1,2,3,4,5,7;
23: 1,2,3,4,5,8; 1,2,3,4,6,7;
24: 1,2,3,4,5,9; 1,2,3,4,6,8; 1,2,3,5,6,7;
25: 1,2,3,4,6,9; 1,2,3,4,7,8; 1,2,3,5,6,8; 1,2,4,5,6,7;
26: 1,2,3,4,7,9; 1,2,3,5,6,9; 1,2,3,5,7,8; 1,2,4,5,6,8; 1,3,4,5,6,7;
27: 1,2,3,4,8,9; 1,2,3,5,7,9; 1,2,3,6,7,8; 1,2,4,5,6,9; 1,2,4,5,7,8; 1,3,4,5,6,8; 2,3,4,5,6,7;
28: 1,2,3,5,8,9; 1,2,3,6,7,9; 1,2,4,5,7,9; 1,2,4,6,7,8; 1,3,4,5,6,9; 1,3,4,5,7,8; 2,3,4,5,6,8;
29: 1,2,3,6,8,9; 1,2,4,5,8,9; 1,2,4,6,7,9; 1,2,5,6,7,8; 1,3,4,5,7,9; 1,3,4,6,7,8; 2,3,4,5,6,9; 2,3,4,5,7,8;
30: 1,2,3,7,8,9; 1,2,4,6,8,9; 1,2,5,6,7,9; 1,3,4,5,8,9; 1,3,4,6,7,9; 1,3,5,6,7,8; 2,3,4,5,7,9; 2,3,4,6,7,8;
31: 1,2,4,7,8,9; 1,2,5,6,8,9; 1,3,4,6,8,9; 1,3,5,6,7,9; 1,4,5,6,7,8; 2,3,4,5,8,9; 2,3,4,6,7,9; 2,3,5,6,7,8;
32: 1,2,5,7,8,9; 1,3,4,7,8,9; 1,3,5,6,8,9; 1,4,5,6,7,9; 2,3,4,6,8,9; 2,3,5,6,7,9; 2,4,5,6,7,8;
33: 1,2,6,7,8,9; 1,3,5,7,8,9; 1,4,5,6,8,9; 2,3,4,7,8,9; 2,3,5,6,8,9; 2,4,5,6,7,9; 3,4,5,6,7,8;
34: 1,3,6,7,8,9; 1,4,5,7,8,9; 2,3,5,7,8,9; 2,4,5,6,8,9; 3,4,5,6,7,9;
35: 1,4,6,7,8,9; 2,3,6,7,8,9; 2,4,5,7,8,9; 3,4,5,6,8,9;
36: 1,5,6,7,8,9; 2,4,6,7,8,9; 3,4,5,7,8,9;
37: 2,5,6,7,8,9; 3,4,6,7,8,9;
38: 3,5,6,7,8,9;
39: 4,5,6,7,8,9;

# Level 1

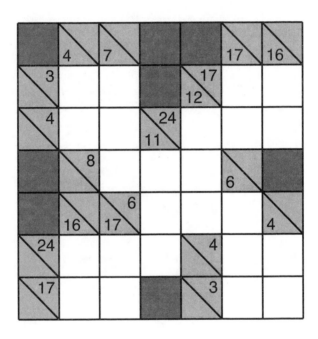

PUZZLE 1

# Level 1

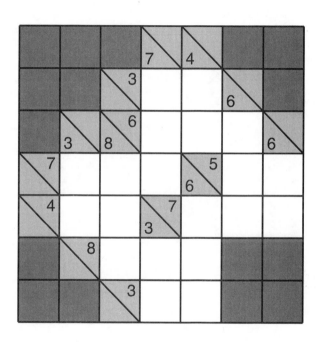

PUZZLE 2

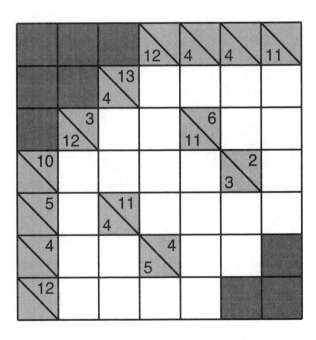

PUZZLE 3

# Level 1

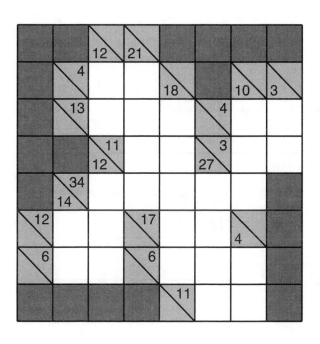

PUZZLE 4

# The Essential Book of KAKURO

PUZZLE 5

# Level 1

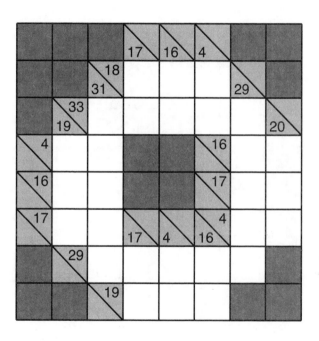

PUZZLE 6

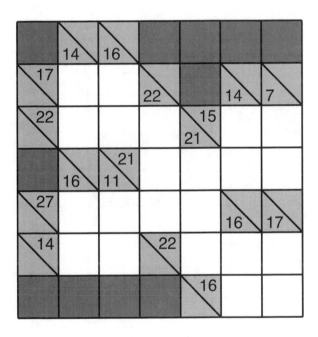

PUZZLE 7

# Level 1

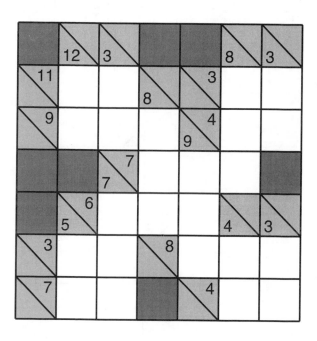

PUZZLE 8

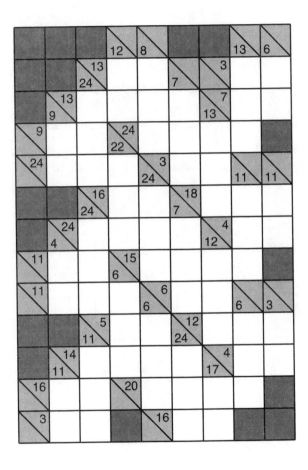

PUZZLE 9

# Level 1

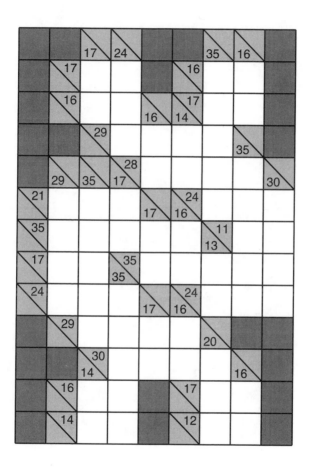

PUZZLE 10

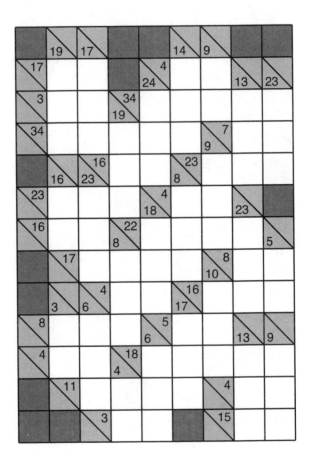

PUZZLE 11

# Level 1

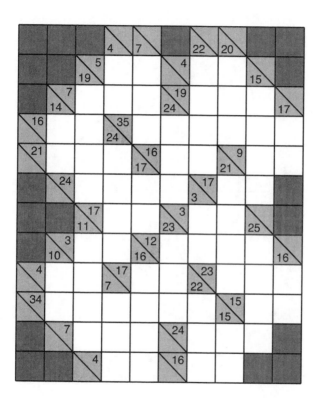

PUZZLE 12

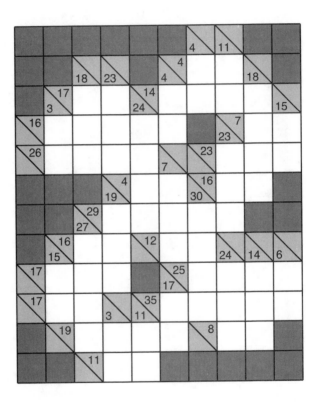

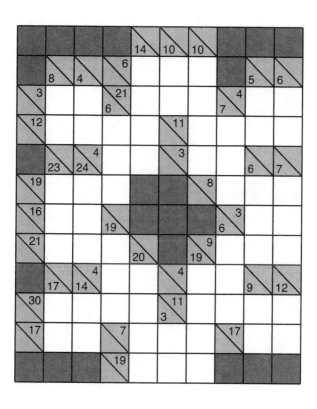

PUZZLE 14

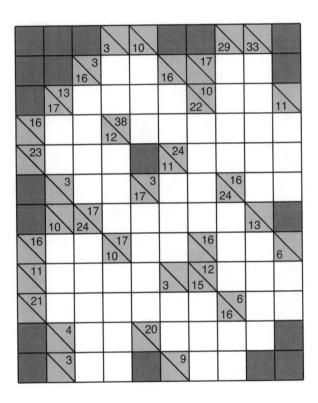

PUZZLE 15

# Level 1

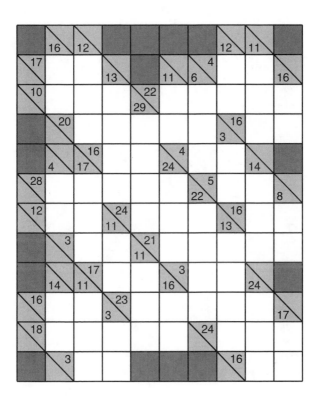

PUZZLE 16

PUZZLE 17

# Level 1

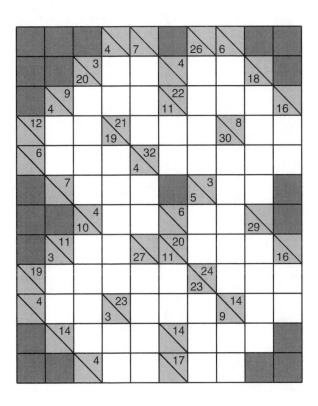

PUZZLE 18

PUZZLE 19

# Level 1

PUZZLE 20

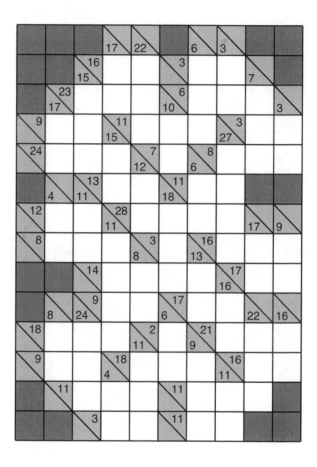

PUZZLE 21

# Level 2

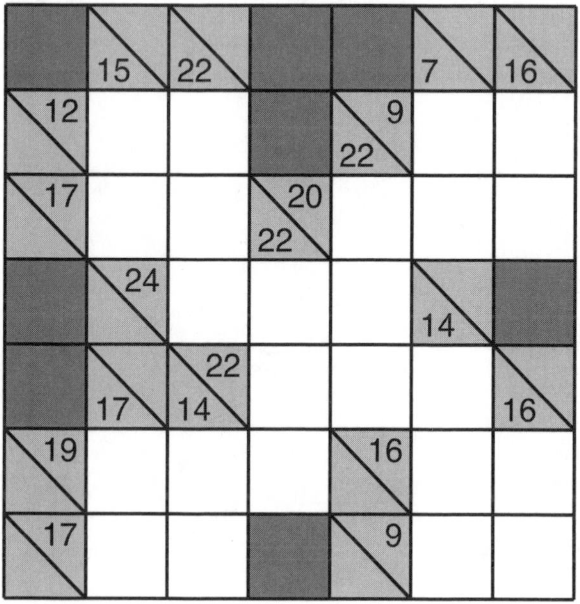


PUZZLE 22

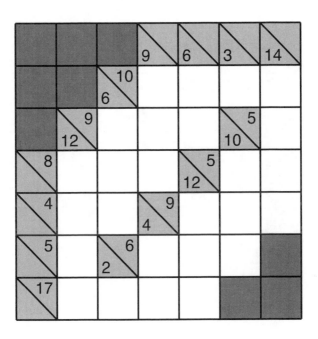

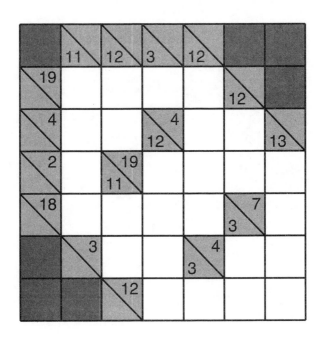

# Level 2

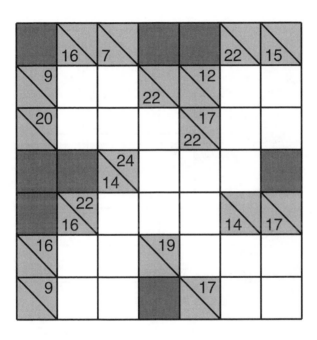

PUZZLE 25

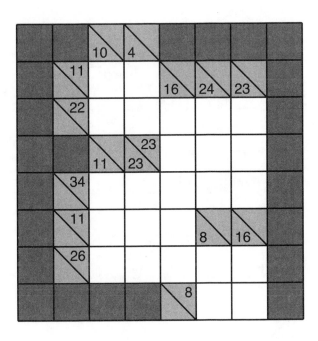

PUZZLE 26

# Level 2

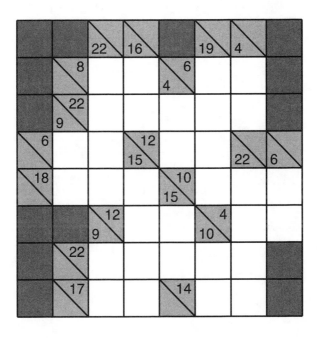

PUZZLE 27

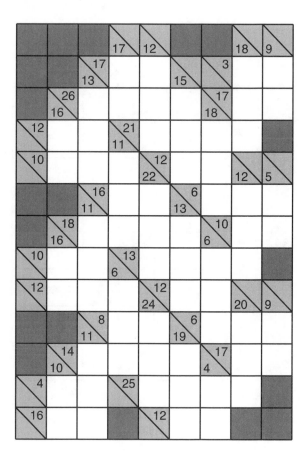

PUZZLE 28

# Level 2

PUZZLE 29

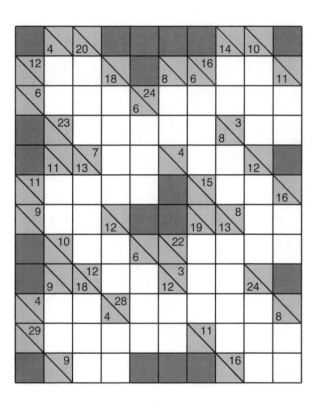

PUZZLE 30

# Level 2

PUZZLE 31

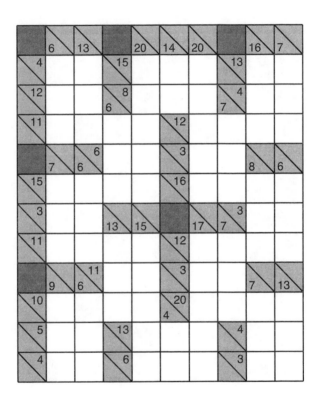

# Level 2

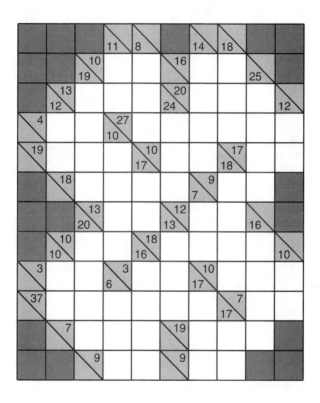

PUZZLE 33

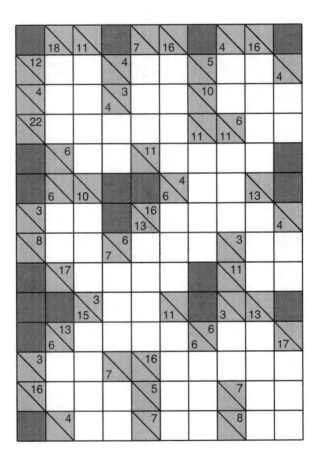

PUZZLE 34

# Level 2

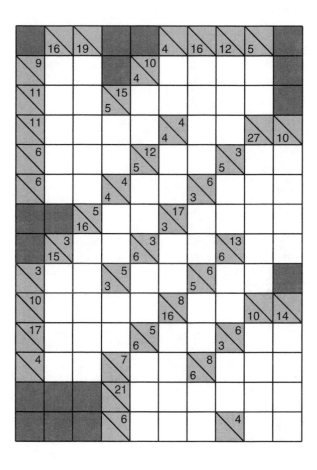

PUZZLE 35

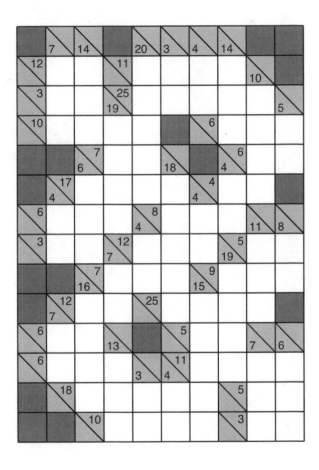

PUZZLE 36

# Level 2

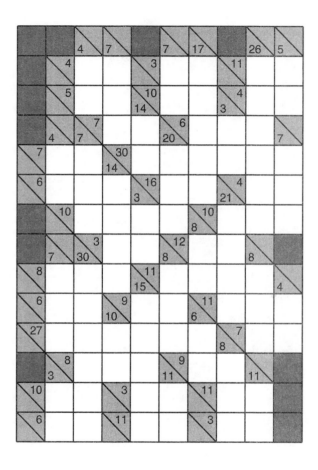

PUZZLE 37

# The Essential Book of KAKURO

PUZZLE 38

# Level 2

PUZZLE 39

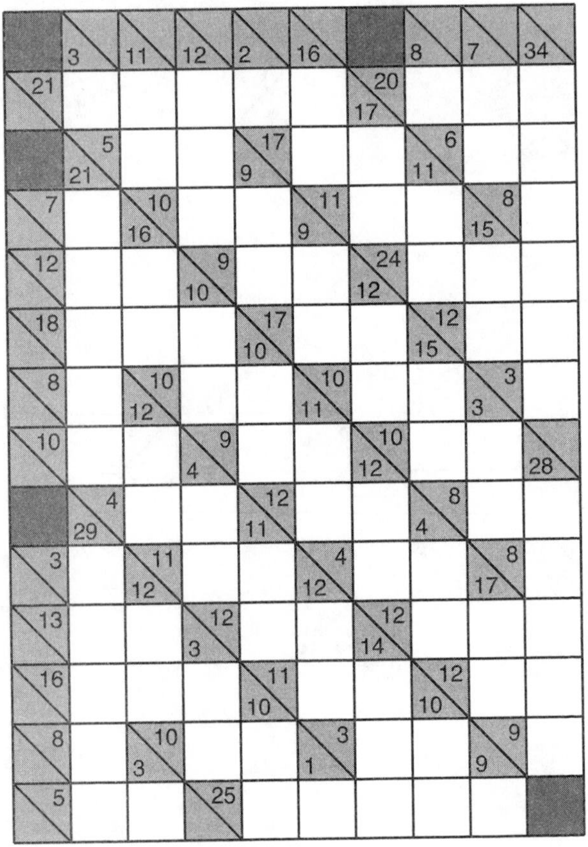

PUZZLE 40

# Level 2

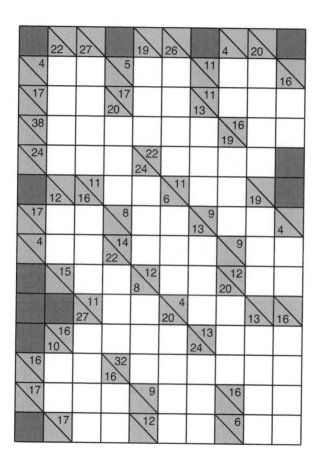

PUZZLE 41

Level 3

# Level 3

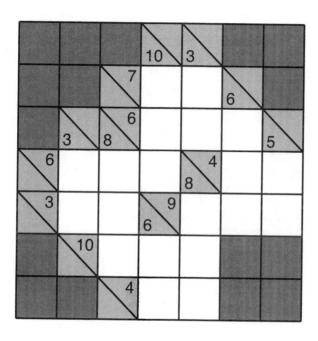

The Essential Book of KAKURO

PUZZLE 43

# Level 3

PUZZLE 44

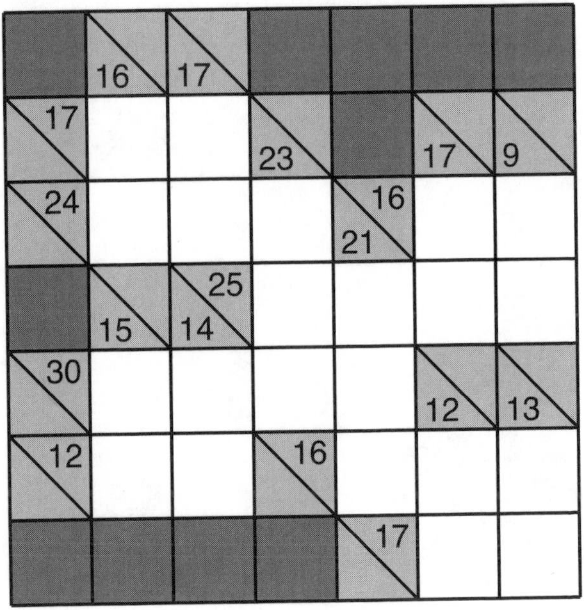


PUZZLE 45

# Level 3

PUZZLE 46

PUZZLE 47

# Level 3

PUZZLE 48

PUZZLE 49

# Level 3

PUZZLE 50

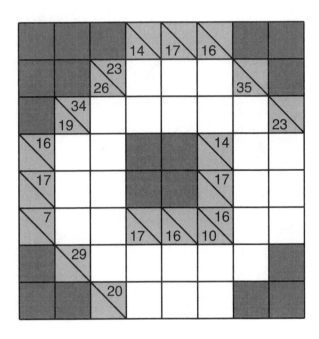

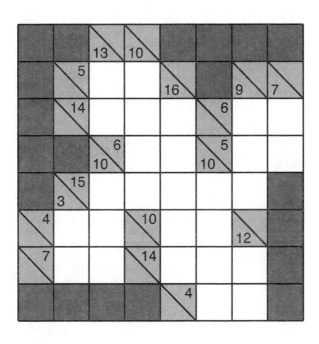

# The Essential Book of KAKURO

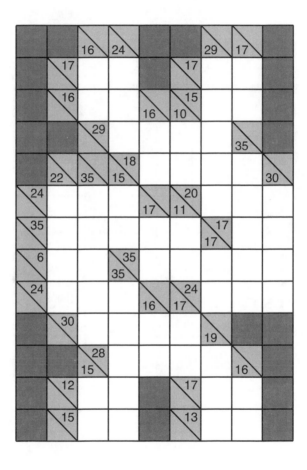

PUZZLE 53

# Level 3

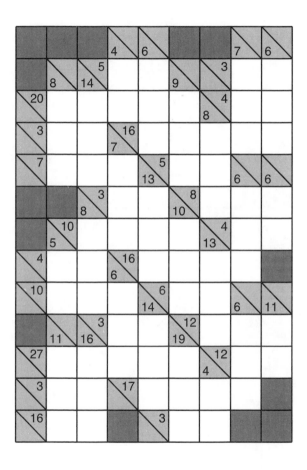

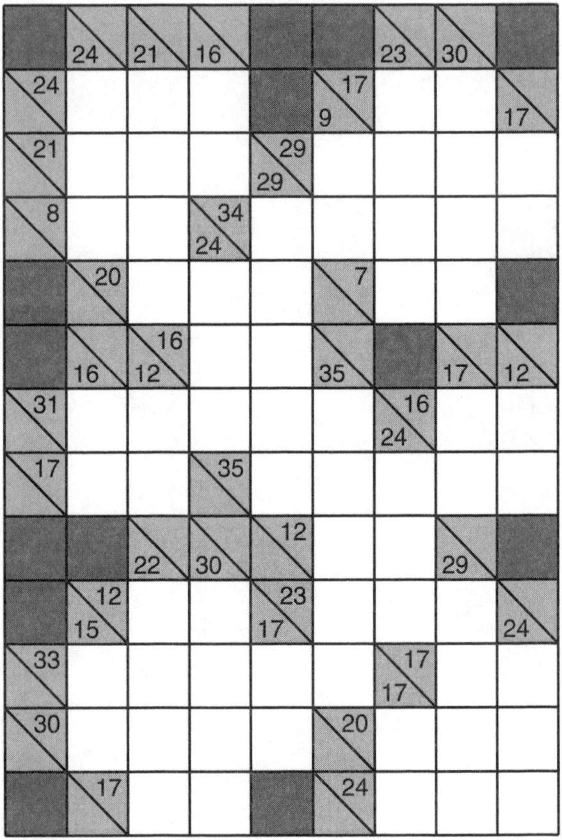

# PUZZLE 55

# Level 3

PUZZLE 56

| | | | | | | | | | |
|---|---|---|---|---|---|---|---|---|---|
| ■ | 23\ | 19\ | ■ | 35\ | 16\ | 35\ | ■ | 22\ | 23\ |
| \16 | | | \20 | | | | \16 | | |
| \12 | | | 24\24 | | | | 18\14 | | |
| \30 | | | | | \30 | | | | |
| ■ | 24\ | 21\17 | | | \6 | | | 16\ | 24\ |
| \27 | | | | | \29 | | | | |
| \15 | | | 21\ | 35\ | ■ | 32\ | 24\17 | | |
| \30 | | | | | \27 | | | | |
| ■ | 24\ | 23\13 | | | \17 | | | 23\ | 24\ |
| \29 | | | | | 14\26 | | | | |
| \14 | | | \20 | | | | \17 | | |
| \16 | | | \24 | | | | \14 | | |

PUZZLE 57

# Level 3

PUZZLE 58

# The Essential Book of KAKURO

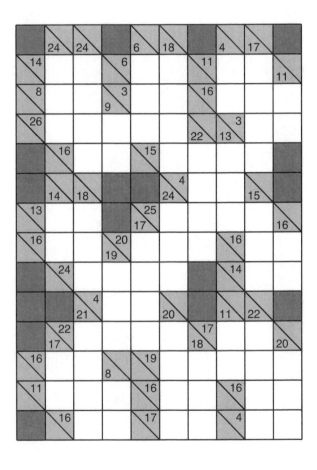

# Level 3

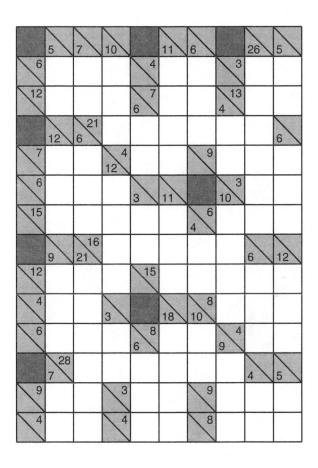

PUZZLE 60

PUZZLE 61

# Level 4

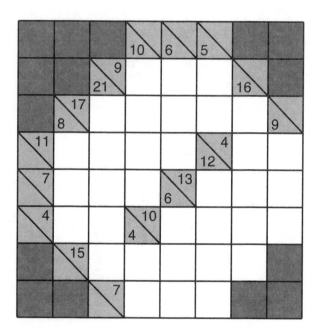

# Level 4

PUZZLE 63

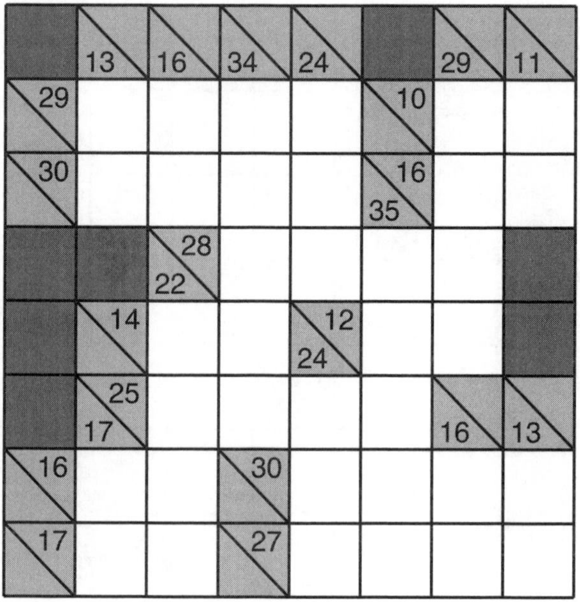


PUZZLE 64

Level 4

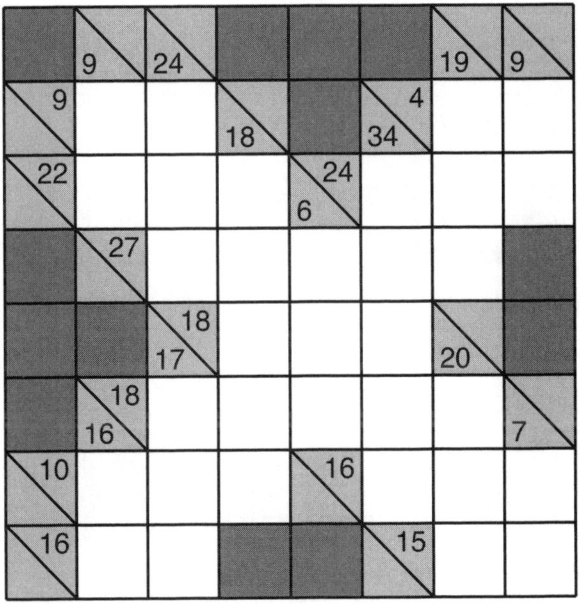

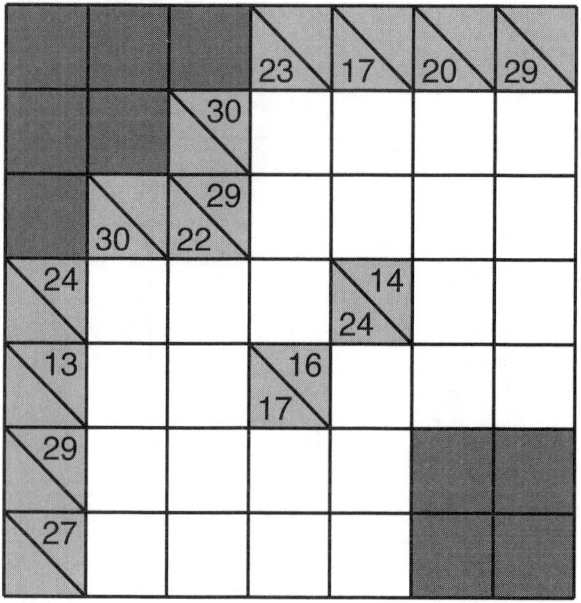


PUZZLE 66

# Level 4

PUZZLE 67

# The Essential Book of KAKURO

# Level 4

| | | | | | | | | |
|---|---|---|---|---|---|---|---|---|
| ■ | 17\ | 20\ | 9\ | ■ | ■ | 10\ | 17\ | ■ |
| \9 | | | | ■ | 10\13 | | | 4\ |
| \24 | | | | 26\11 | | | | |
| \4 | | | 9\18 | | | | | |
| ■ | \23 | | | | \4 | | | ■ |
| ■ | 5\ | 15\9 | | | 26\ | ■ | 16\ | 11\ |
| \16 | | | | | | 7\14 | | |
| \10 | | | \28 | | | | | |
| ■ | ■ | 13\ | 25\ | \12 | | | 15\ | ■ |
| ■ | 17\6 | | | 4\10 | | | | 21\ |
| \18 | | | | | | 11\17 | | |
| \20 | | | | | \8 | | | |
| ■ | \16 | | | ■ | \18 | | | |

PUZZLE 69

PUZZLE 70

Level 4

| | | | | | | | | |
|---|---|---|---|---|---|---|---|---|
| ■ | ■ | 17\ | 16\ | ■ | 17\ | 10\ | 18\ | 29\ |
| ■ | \15 | | | \13 | | | | |
| ■ | 7\8 | | | 27\28 | | | | |
| \3 | | | 8\17 | | | | | |
| \17 | | | | | \19 | | | |
| ■ | 4\ | 9\14 | | | 21\ | ■ | 16\ | 11\ |
| \26 | | | | | | 20\16 | | |
| \3 | | | \24 | | | | | |
| ■ | 22\ | 10\ | 29\ | \7 | | | 26\ | 7\ |
| \9 | | | | 15\25 | | | | |
| \34 | | | | | | 13\5 | | |
| \27 | | | | | \10 | | | ■ |
| \15 | | | | | \17 | | | ■ |

PUZZLE 71

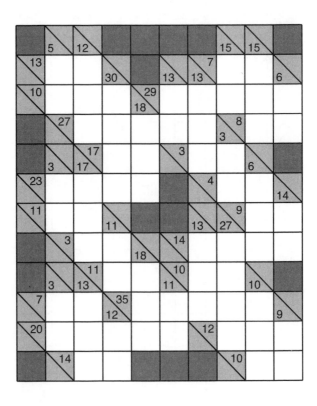

PUZZLE 72

# Level 4

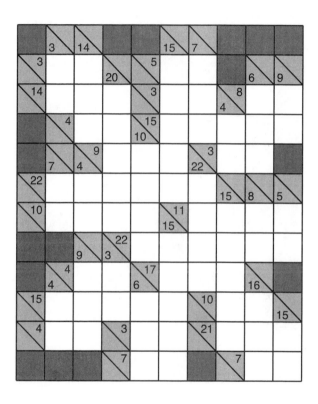

PUZZLE 73

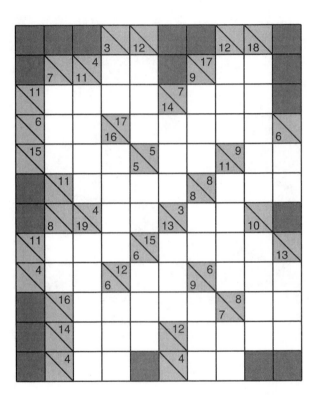

# Level 4

PUZZLE 75

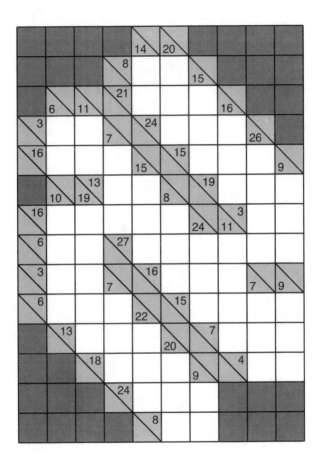

PUZZLE 76

# Level 4

PUZZLE 77

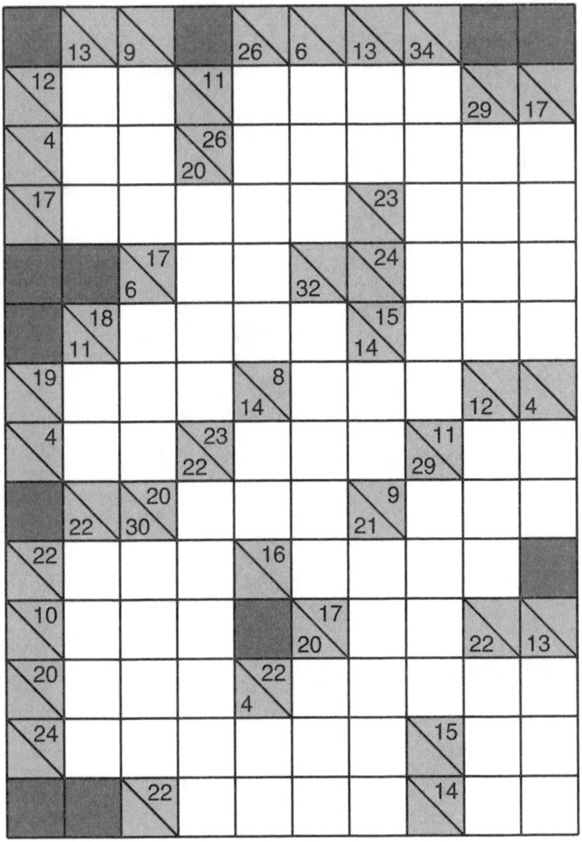

13 9 26 6 13 34
12 11 29 17
4 26 20
17 23
17 6 32 24
18 11 15 14
19 8 14 12 4
4 23 22 11 29
20 22 30 9 21
22 16
10 17 20 22 13
20 22 4
24 15
22 14


PUZZLE 78

## Level 4

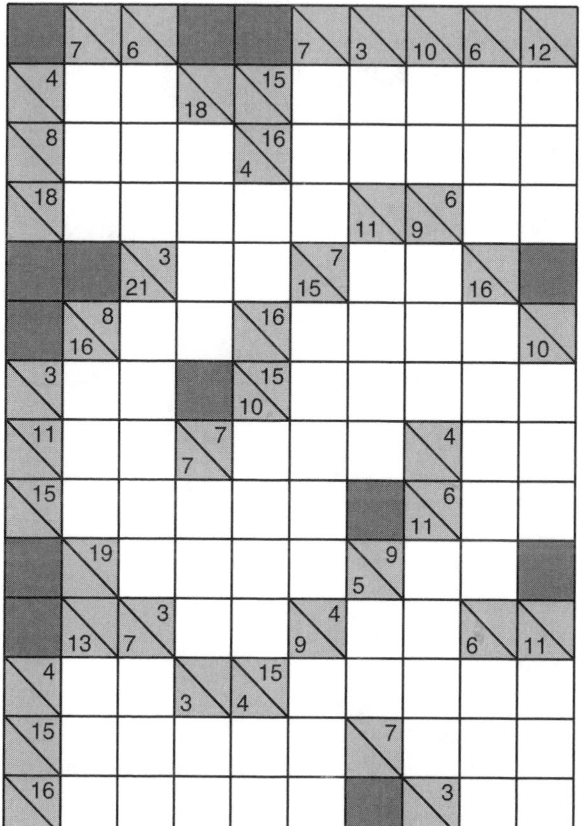

PUZZLE 79

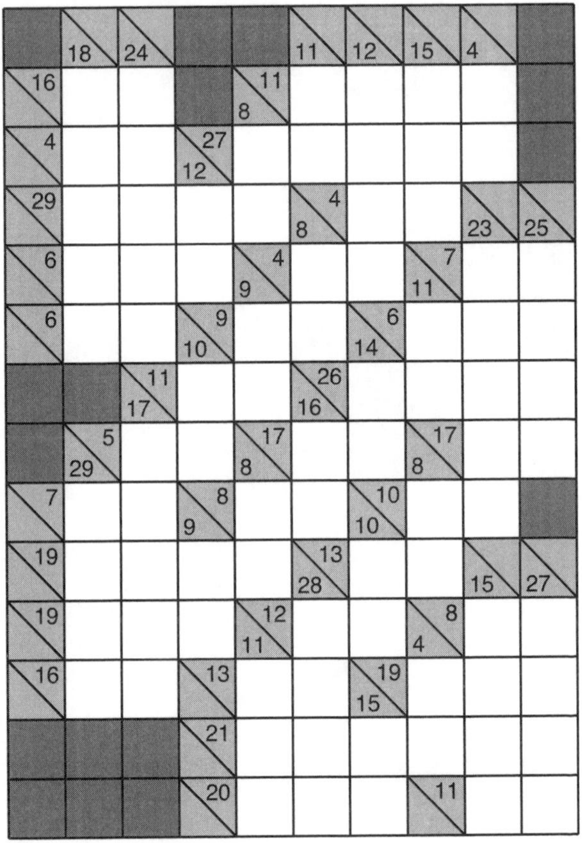
18 24 11 12 15 4
16 11 8
4 27 12
29 4 8 23 25
6 4 9 7 11
6 9 10 6 14
11 17 26 16
5 29 17 8 17 8
7 8 9 10 10
19 13 28 15 27
19 12 11 8 4
16 13 19 15
21
20 11

PUZZLE 80

# Level 4

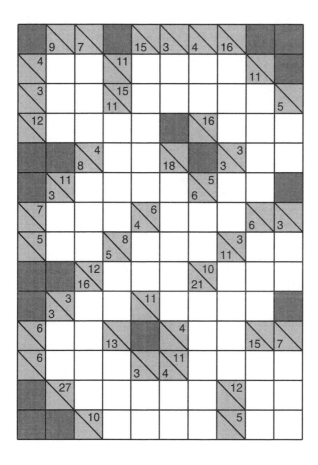

# Level 5

# Level 5

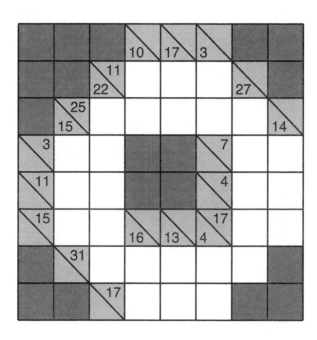

PUZZLE 82

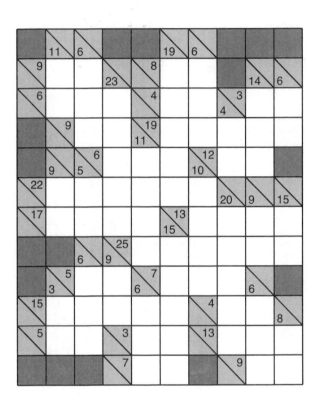

# Level 5

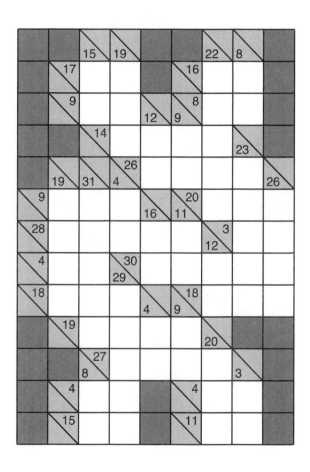

PUZZLE 84

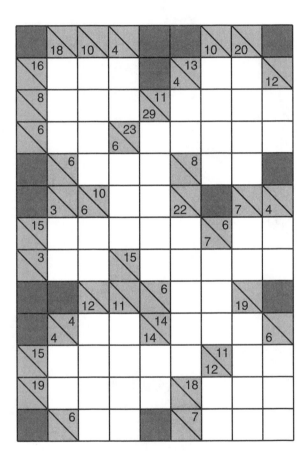

PUZZLE 85

# Level 5

PUZZLE 86

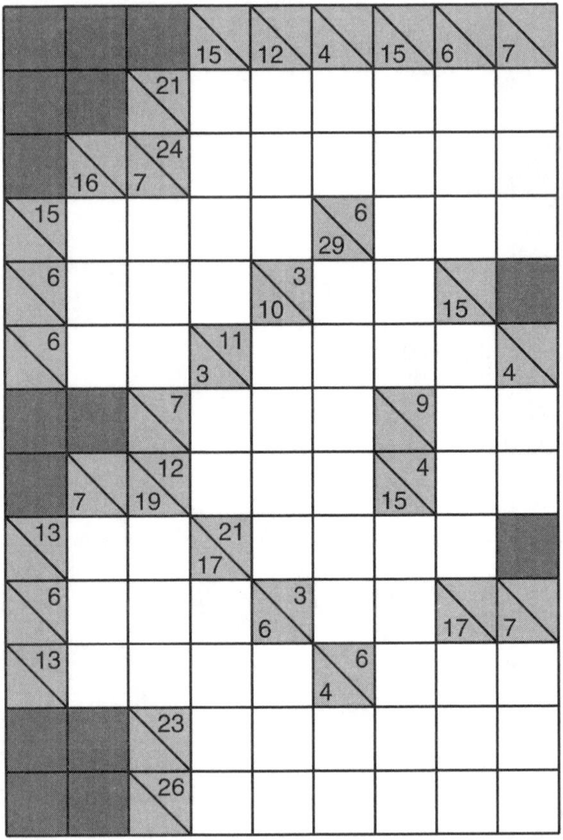

## PUZZLE 87

## Level 5

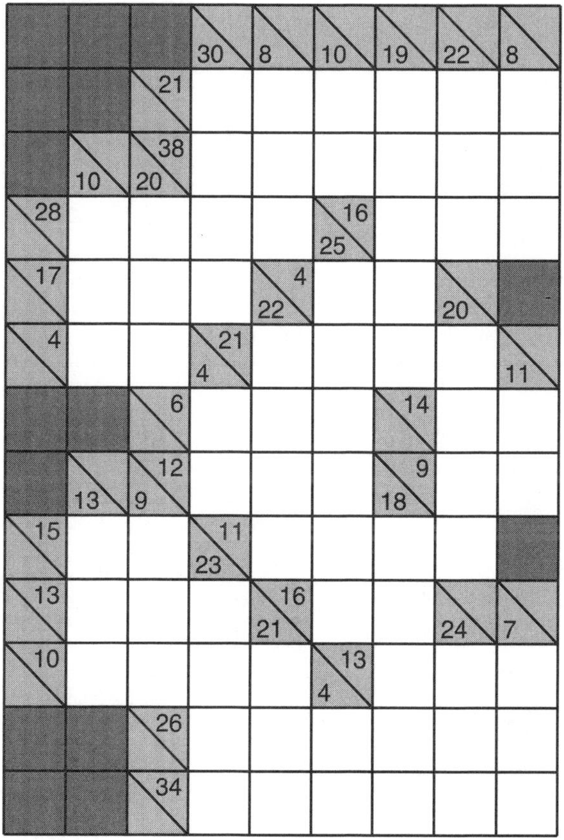


PUZZLE 88

The Essential Book of KAKURO

PUZZLE 89

# Level 5

PUZZLE 90

| | | | | | | | | |
|---|---|---|---|---|---|---|---|---|
| ■ | 28\ | 30\ | ■ | 17\ | 35\ | ■ | 22\ | 24\ |
| \13 | | | \13 | | | \15 | | |
| \17 | | | 29\17 | | | 23\17 | | |
| \23 | | | | \27 | | | | |
| \21 | | | | 15\17 | | | 16\ | 24\ |
| ■ | 18\ | 22\39 | | | | | | |
| \30 | | | | | 15\ | 29\16 | | |
| \16 | | | 23\ | 33\28 | | | | |
| \38 | | | | | | | 30\ | 28\ |
| ■ | 24\ | 19\16 | | | \19 | | | |
| \23 | | | | | 9\23 | | | |
| \17 | | | \16 | | | \13 | | |
| \13 | | | \10 | | | \16 | | |

PUZZLE 91

Level 5

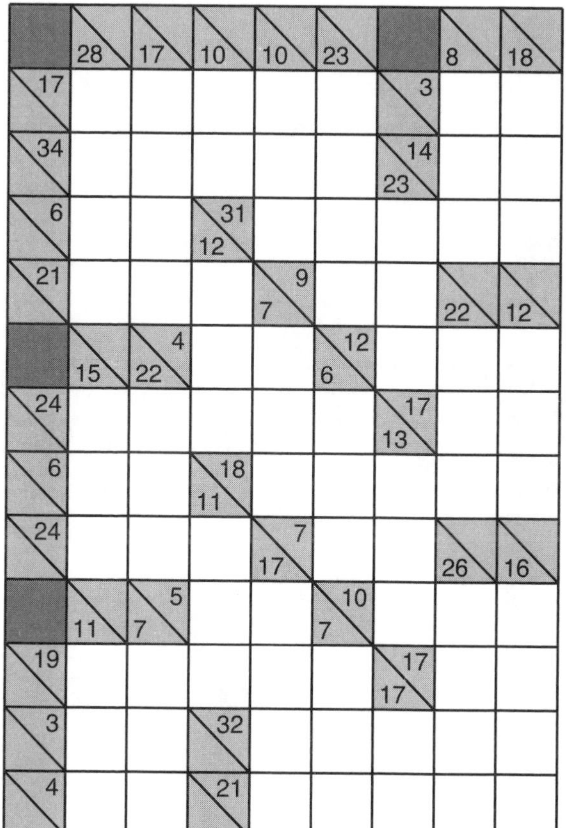

PUZZLE 92

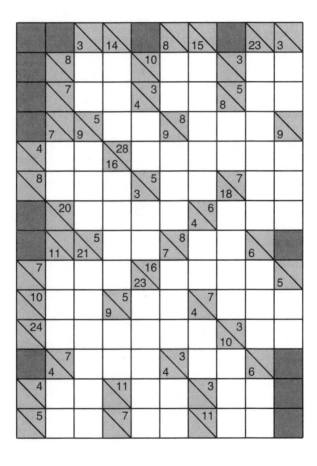

# Level 5

PUZZLE 94

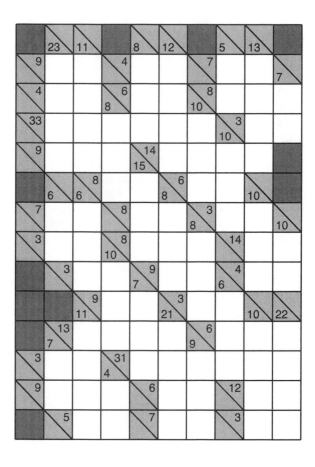

PUZZLE 95

# Level 5

PUZZLE 96

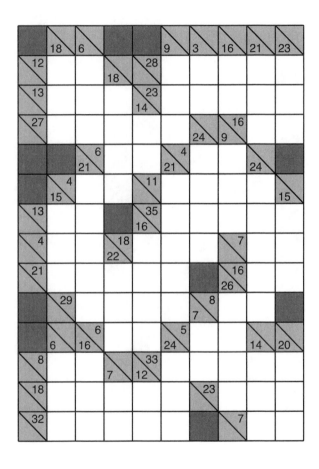

# Level 5

PUZZLE 98

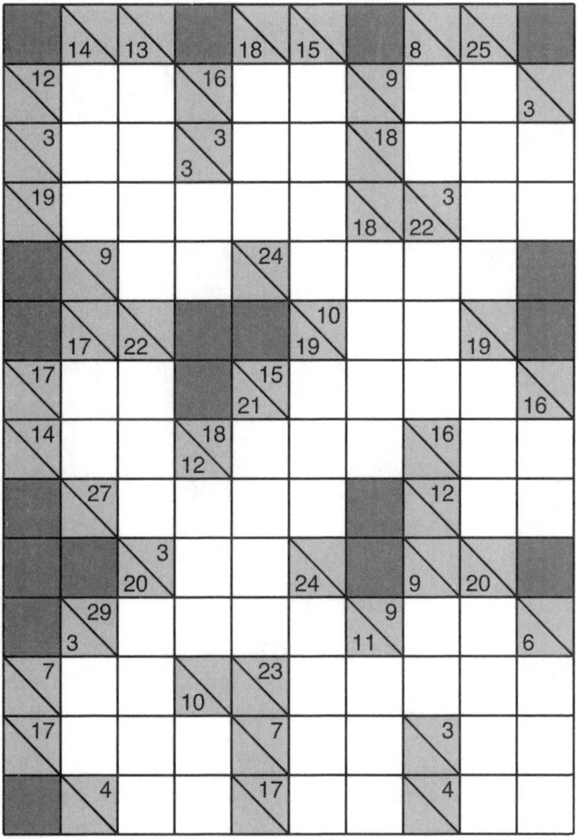
14 13 18 15 8 25
12 16 9 3
3 3 3 18
19 18 3 22
9 24
17 22 10 19 19
17 15 21 16
14 18 12 16
27 12
3 20 24 9 20
29 3 9 11 6
7 10 23
17 7 3
4 17 4

PUZZLE 99

# Level 5

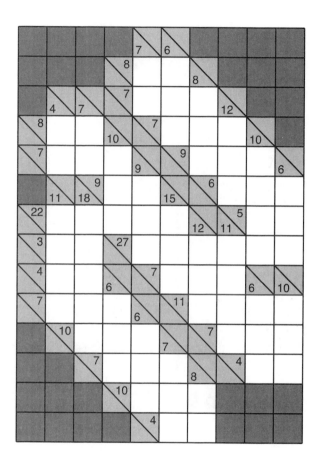

PUZZLE 100

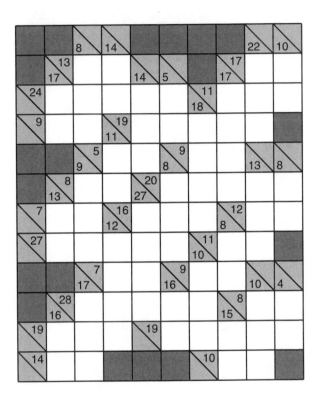

# Answers

# ANSWERS

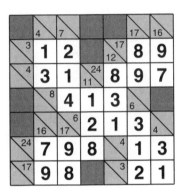

PUZZLE 1

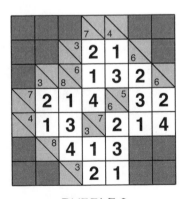

PUZZLE 2

# ANSWERS

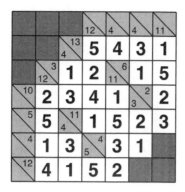

PUZZLE 3

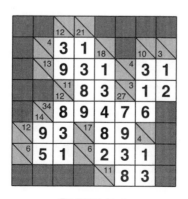

PUZZLE 4

# ANSWERS

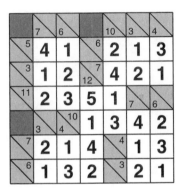

PUZZLE 5

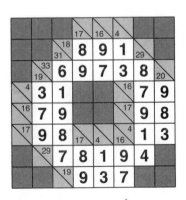

PUZZLE 6

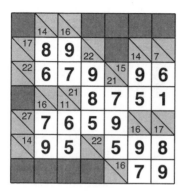

PUZZLE 7

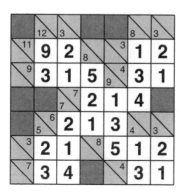

PUZZLE 8

# ANSWERS

PUZZLE 9

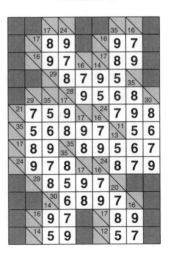

PUZZLE 10

# ANSWERS

PUZZLE 11

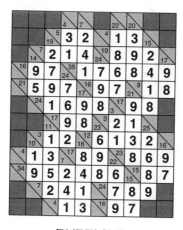

PUZZLE 12

# ANSWERS

PUZZLE 13

PUZZLE 14

# ANSWERS

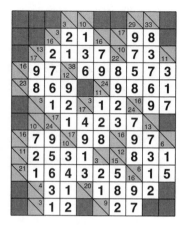

PUZZLE 15

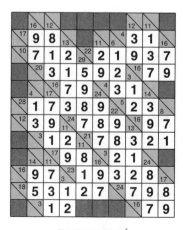

PUZZLE 16

# ANSWERS

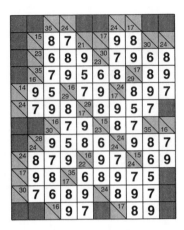

## PUZZLE 17

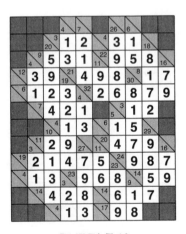

## PUZZLE 18

# ANSWERS

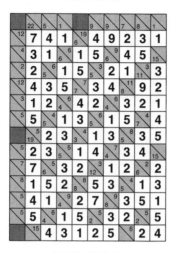

PUZZLE 19

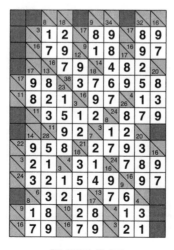

PUZZLE 20

# ANSWERS

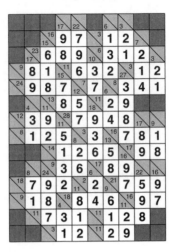

PUZZLE 21

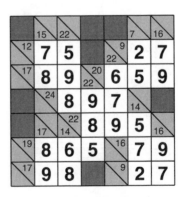

PUZZLE 22

# ANSWERS

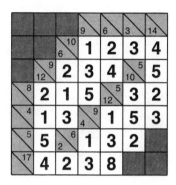

PUZZLE 23

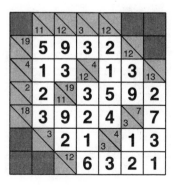

PUZZLE 24

# ANSWERS

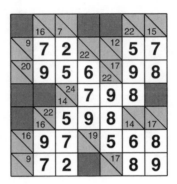

PUZZLE 25

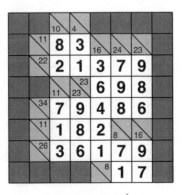

PUZZLE 26

# ANSWERS

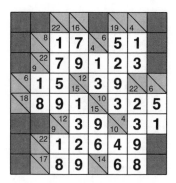

## PUZZLE 27

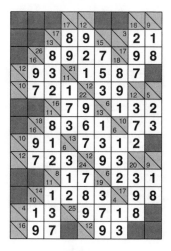

## PUZZLE 28

# ANSWERS

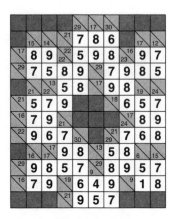

PUZZLE 29

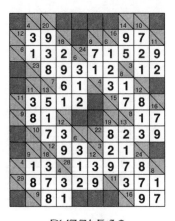

PUZZLE 30

# ANSWERS

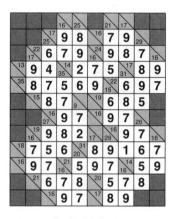

PUZZLE 31

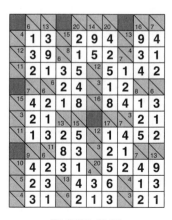

PUZZLE 32

# ANSWERS

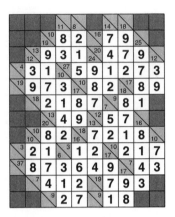

PUZZLE 33

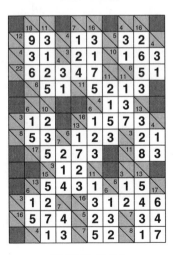

PUZZLE 34

# ANSWERS

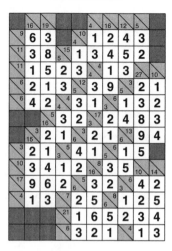

PUZZLE 35

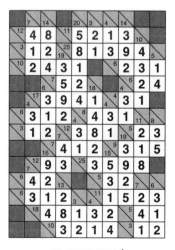

PUZZLE 36

# ANSWERS

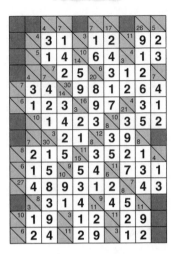

PUZZLE 37

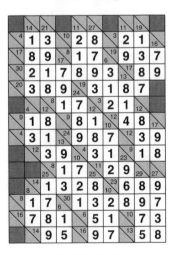

PUZZLE 38

# ANSWERS

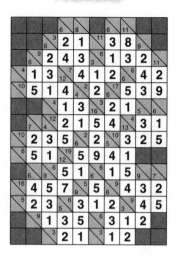

## PUZZLE 39

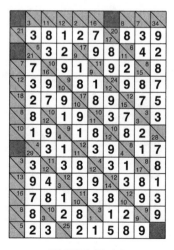

## PUZZLE 40

# ANSWERS

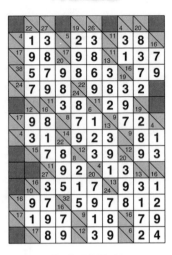

PUZZLE 41

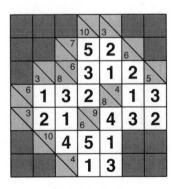

PUZZLE 42

# ANSWERS

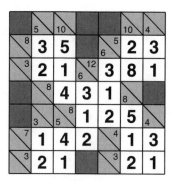

PUZZLE 43

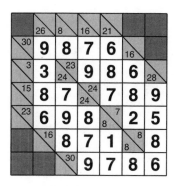

PUZZLE 44

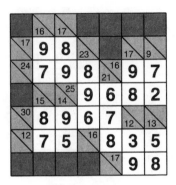

PUZZLE 45

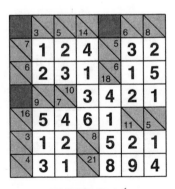

PUZZLE 46

# ANSWERS

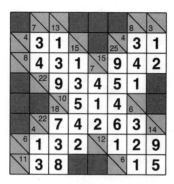

PUZZLE 47

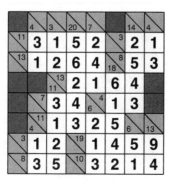

PUZZLE 48

# ANSWERS

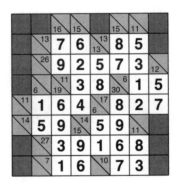

PUZZLE 49

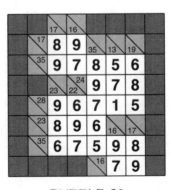

PUZZLE 50

# ANSWERS

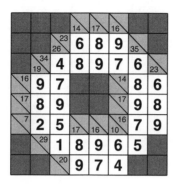

PUZZLE 51

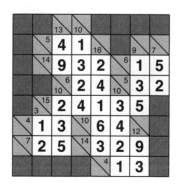

PUZZLE 52

# ANSWERS

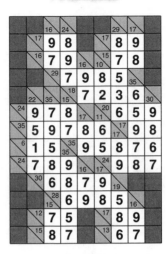

PUZZLE 53

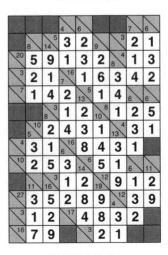

PUZZLE 54

# ANSWERS

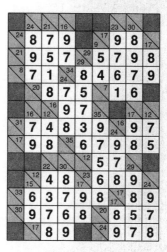

PUZZLE 55

PUZZLE 56

# ANSWERS

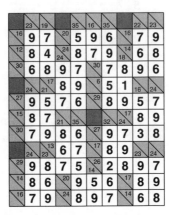

PUZZLE 57

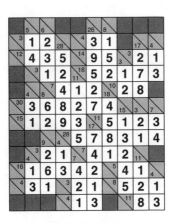

PUZZLE 58

ANSWERS

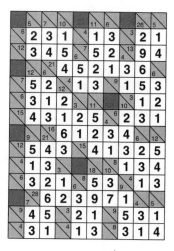

PUZZLE 59

PUZZLE 60

# ANSWERS

PUZZLE 61

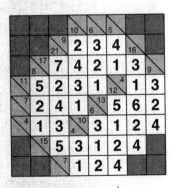

PUZZLE 62

# ANSWERS

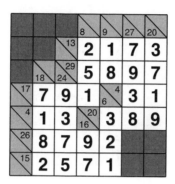

PUZZLE 63

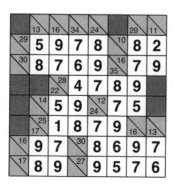

PUZZLE 64

# ANSWERS

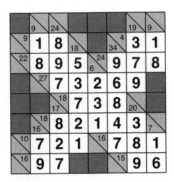

PUZZLE 65

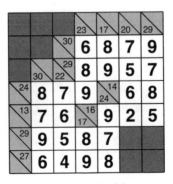

PUZZLE 66

# ANSWERS

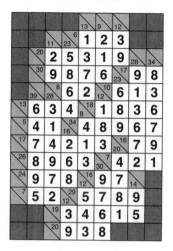

PUZZLE 67

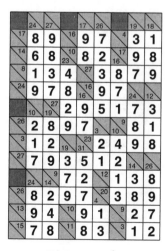

PUZZLE 68

# ANSWERS

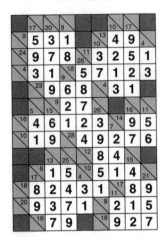

PUZZLE 69

PUZZLE 70

# ANSWERS

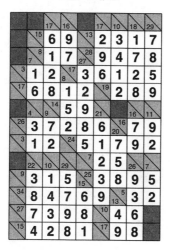

PUZZLE 71

PUZZLE 72

# ANSWERS

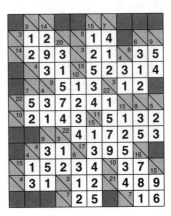

PUZZLE 73

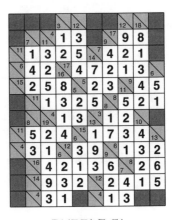

PUZZLE 74

# ANSWERS

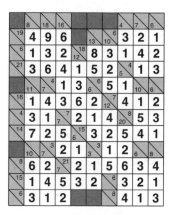

PUZZLE 75

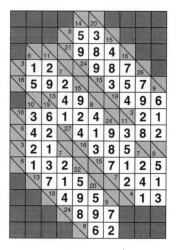

PUZZLE 76

ANSWERS

PUZZLE 77

PUZZLE 78

# ANSWERS

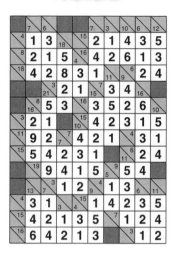

PUZZLE 79

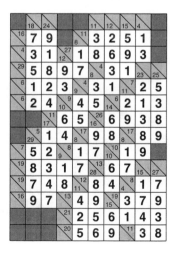

PUZZLE 80

# ANSWERS

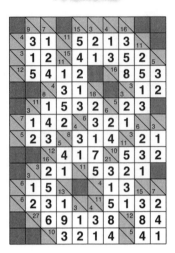

PUZZLE 81

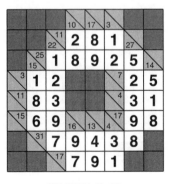

PUZZLE 82

# ANSWERS

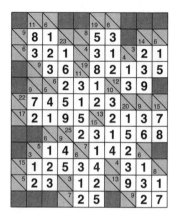

PUZZLE 83

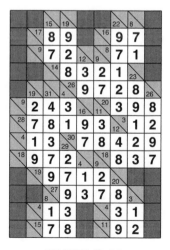

PUZZLE 84

# ANSWERS

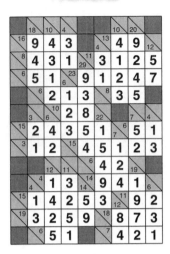

PUZZLE 85

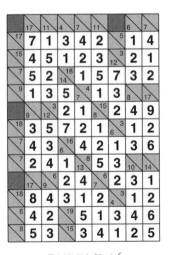

PUZZLE 86

# ANSWERS

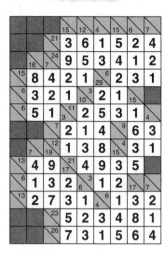

## PUZZLE 87

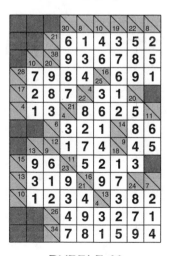

## PUZZLE 88

# ANSWERS

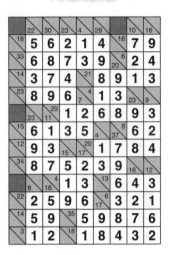

PUZZLE 89

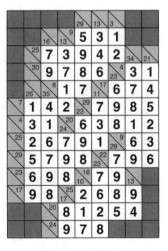

PUZZLE 90

# ANSWERS

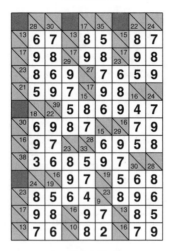

## PUZZLE 91

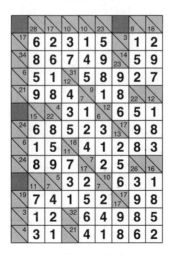

## PUZZLE 92

# ANSWERS

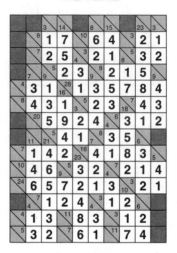

PUZZLE 93

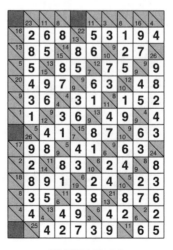

PUZZLE 94

# ANSWERS

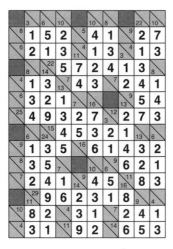

PUZZLE 95

PUZZLE 96

# ANSWERS

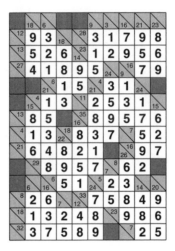

PUZZLE 97

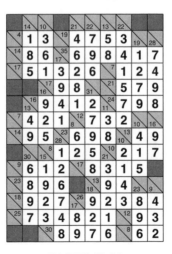

PUZZLE 98

# ANSWERS

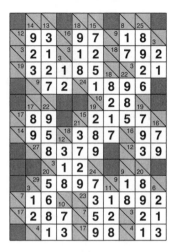

PUZZLE 99

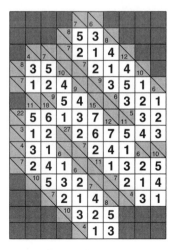

PUZZLE 100

# ANSWERS

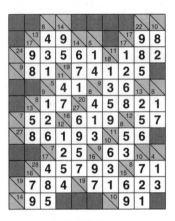

PUZZLE 101

# Turn the page for a bonus taste of Su Doku, the number puzzle phenomenon that swept the world!

The following twelve puzzles are just a tantalizing taste of *The Essential Book of Su Doku* by Pete Sinden, published by Atria Books and available in bookstores everywhere.

Like Kakuro, Su Doku is a number-placement puzzle based on a grid, typically 9 squares by 9, giving 81 squares in all. The puzzle is further divided (by bold gridlines) into 9 boxes or "regions," each a square measuring 3 squares by 3. Figures from 1 to 9 (known as "givens") are already inserted in some of the squares; to complete the puzzle, a player must insert the missing numbers so that each row, each column and each region contains the numbers 1 to 9 once and once only, without any repeats. (If you get stuck, you'll find the solutions at the end.)

## Puzzle 1

|   |   | 1 |   | 7 | 8 |   | 5 |   |
|---|---|---|---|---|---|---|---|---|
| 7 | 8 | 2 |   |   | 9 | 4 |   |   |
| 5 |   |   | 1 |   |   |   |   |   |
|   |   | 8 | 7 |   |   |   | 6 |   |
| 3 |   | 7 | 8 |   | 1 | 2 |   | 4 |
|   | 1 |   |   |   | 3 | 5 |   |   |
|   |   |   |   |   | 2 |   |   | 5 |
|   |   | 5 | 6 |   |   | 9 | 4 | 2 |
|   | 4 |   | 3 | 8 |   | 6 |   |   |

## Puzzle 2

| 7 |   |   |   | 2 |   | 8 |   | 5 |
|---|---|---|---|---|---|---|---|---|
|   |   | 8 |   | 6 |   |   | 3 | 9 |
| 4 |   | 9 |   |   |   |   |   |   |
| 1 |   | 3 | 2 |   |   |   |   |   |
| 8 |   | 2 | 3 | 9 | 1 | 5 |   | 4 |
|   |   |   |   |   | 5 | 3 |   | 1 |
|   |   |   |   |   |   | 1 |   | 8 |
| 3 | 8 |   |   | 1 |   | 4 |   |   |
| 9 |   | 6 |   | 7 |   |   |   | 3 |

## Puzzle 3

| | | 1 | | 5 | | 7 | 6 | 8 |
|---|---|---|---|---|---|---|---|---|
| 9 | 6 | | | | 7 | | | |
| 7 | 5 | | | 6 | | 4 | | |
| 3 | | 6 | 9 | | | | | |
| | | 9 | 1 | | 5 | 8 | | |
| | | | | | 8 | 2 | | 4 |
| | | 4 | | 9 | | | 1 | 5 |
| | | | 5 | | | | 8 | 2 |
| 6 | 9 | 5 | | | 1 | | 3 | |

## Puzzle 4

| | 4 | | | | | | 6 | |
|---|---|---|---|---|---|---|---|---|
| | | 6 | | 9 | | 2 | | |
| 1 | | | 7 | 8 | 6 | | | 4 |
| 6 | | | 5 | | 9 | | | 8 |
| | 5 | 8 | | 7 | | 9 | 3 | |
| 9 | | | 3 | | 8 | | | 7 |
| 8 | | | 9 | 3 | 7 | | | 5 |
| | | 7 | | 5 | | 3 | | |
| | 1 | | | | | | 4 | |

| 6 |   | 2 | 3 |   |   | 8 |   | 7 |
|---|---|---|---|---|---|---|---|---|
|   |   | 3 |   |   | 1 | 9 | 5 |   |
| 1 | 7 | 9 |   |   |   |   |   | 4 |
|   |   | 8 |   |   |   |   | 7 | 9 |
|   |   |   | 8 |   | 7 |   |   |   |
| 7 | 1 |   |   |   |   | 6 |   |   |
| 3 |   |   |   |   |   | 7 | 9 | 2 |
|   | 8 | 1 | 6 |   |   | 3 |   |   |
| 4 |   | 7 |   |   | 5 | 1 |   | 8 |

# Puzzle 6

| | | | 7 | | | 5 | | 1 |
|---|---|---|---|---|---|---|---|---|
| | | | | 6 | 5 | 9 | 7 | |
| | | 7 | | | 9 | 4 | | 2 |
| 9 | | 5 | | | | 7 | 1 | |
| | 6 | 2 | | 4 | | 3 | 8 | |
| | 7 | 8 | | | | 2 | | 9 |
| 4 | | 3 | 5 | | | 1 | | |
| | 5 | 9 | 1 | 7 | | | | |
| 7 | | 1 | | | 2 | | | |

## Puzzle 7

| 1 | 4 | 5 |   |   |   |   |   | 3 |
|---|---|---|---|---|---|---|---|---|
|   |   | 9 | 2 |   | 7 |   |   | 1 |
| 3 |   |   |   |   | 1 | 6 |   | 8 |
|   | 3 |   | 9 |   |   |   | 7 |   |
| 9 | 1 |   |   |   |   |   | 8 | 2 |
|   | 5 |   |   |   | 8 |   | 6 |   |
| 5 |   | 3 | 8 |   |   |   |   | 6 |
| 2 |   |   | 7 |   | 6 | 8 |   |   |
| 4 |   |   |   |   |   | 2 | 1 | 7 |

## Puzzle 8

|   |   |   | 1 |   | 3 | 5 |   |   |
|---|---|---|---|---|---|---|---|---|
| 7 | 2 |   |   | 6 |   |   |   | 3 |
| 8 | 3 |   |   |   | 9 |   | 2 |   |
| 6 |   |   |   |   | 8 |   | 9 | 2 |
|   | 8 | 7 |   |   |   | 6 | 3 |   |
| 3 | 9 |   | 4 |   |   |   |   | 5 |
|   | 7 |   | 5 |   |   |   | 6 | 8 |
| 9 |   |   |   | 3 |   |   | 7 | 1 |
|   |   | 6 | 2 |   | 7 |   |   |   |

## Puzzle 9

| 9 |   |   | 8 |   | 2 |   |   |   |
|---|---|---|---|---|---|---|---|---|
|   | 6 | 1 |   |   | 9 | 2 |   |   |
|   |   |   | 5 |   | 4 | 7 | 6 | 9 |
|   |   | 6 |   |   | 5 |   |   |   |
|   | 9 | 8 | 6 |   | 3 | 1 | 2 |   |
|   |   |   | 1 |   |   | 3 |   |   |
| 8 | 5 | 3 | 4 |   | 1 |   |   |   |
|   |   | 4 | 2 |   |   | 9 | 5 |   |
|   |   |   | 7 |   | 6 |   |   | 8 |

## Puzzle 10

|   |   | 4 |   |   |   | 3 |   | 5 |
|---|---|---|---|---|---|---|---|---|
|   |   | 6 | 5 | 7 |   |   | 1 |   |
| 5 |   |   |   | 4 |   | 2 | 8 | 7 |
| 6 |   | 9 |   | 3 |   |   |   |   |
|   | 8 |   | 7 |   | 5 |   | 9 |   |
|   |   |   |   | 2 |   | 1 |   | 6 |
| 2 | 9 | 8 |   | 5 |   |   |   | 1 |
|   | 6 |   |   | 1 | 2 | 7 |   |   |
| 7 |   | 3 |   |   |   | 5 |   |   |

## Puzzle 11

| 5 |   |   | 7 | 1 |   |   |   |   |
|---|---|---|---|---|---|---|---|---|
|   |   | 6 |   | 2 |   | 7 | 8 |   |
|   |   |   | 4 | 8 |   | 2 | 9 |   |
| 8 |   | 7 |   | 9 |   | 5 | 1 |   |
|   | 5 | 9 |   |   |   | 4 | 7 |   |
|   | 3 | 4 |   | 7 |   | 8 |   | 9 |
|   | 2 | 1 |   | 5 | 7 |   |   |   |
|   | 4 | 8 |   | 6 |   | 9 |   |   |
|   |   |   |   | 4 | 3 |   |   | 6 |

## Puzzle 12

|   |   |   | 8 |   | 6 | 1 |   | 5 |
|---|---|---|---|---|---|---|---|---|
| 6 |   | 2 |   |   |   |   |   | 9 |
|   | 5 | 9 |   |   | 1 |   | 6 | 3 |
|   | 6 | 1 |   |   | 5 |   |   |   |
| 3 |   |   | 6 |   | 7 |   |   | 2 |
|   |   |   | 4 |   |   | 5 | 1 |   |
| 7 | 3 |   | 1 |   |   | 6 | 5 |   |
| 1 |   |   |   |   |   | 7 |   | 4 |
| 5 |   | 6 | 7 |   | 8 |   |   |   |

# Solutions 1–12

**1**

| 4 | 6 | 1 | 2 | 7 | 8 | 3 | 5 | 9 |
|---|---|---|---|---|---|---|---|---|
| 7 | 8 | 2 | 5 | 3 | 9 | 4 | 1 | 6 |
| 5 | 9 | 3 | 1 | 4 | 6 | 7 | 2 | 8 |
| 9 | 2 | 8 | 7 | 5 | 4 | 1 | 6 | 3 |
| 3 | 5 | 7 | 8 | 6 | 1 | 2 | 9 | 4 |
| 6 | 1 | 4 | 9 | 2 | 3 | 5 | 8 | 7 |
| 1 | 7 | 6 | 4 | 9 | 2 | 8 | 3 | 5 |
| 8 | 3 | 5 | 6 | 1 | 7 | 9 | 4 | 2 |
| 2 | 4 | 9 | 3 | 8 | 5 | 6 | 7 | 1 |

**2**

| 7 | 6 | 1 | 9 | 2 | 3 | 8 | 4 | 5 |
|---|---|---|---|---|---|---|---|---|
| 5 | 2 | 8 | 1 | 6 | 4 | 7 | 3 | 9 |
| 4 | 3 | 9 | 8 | 5 | 7 | 6 | 1 | 2 |
| 1 | 5 | 3 | 2 | 4 | 6 | 9 | 8 | 7 |
| 8 | 7 | 2 | 3 | 9 | 1 | 5 | 6 | 4 |
| 6 | 9 | 4 | 7 | 8 | 5 | 3 | 2 | 1 |
| 2 | 4 | 5 | 6 | 3 | 9 | 1 | 7 | 8 |
| 3 | 8 | 7 | 5 | 1 | 2 | 4 | 9 | 6 |
| 9 | 1 | 6 | 4 | 7 | 8 | 2 | 5 | 3 |

**3**

| 4 | 3 | 1 | 2 | 5 | 9 | 7 | 6 | 8 |
|---|---|---|---|---|---|---|---|---|
| 9 | 6 | 2 | 4 | 8 | 7 | 1 | 5 | 3 |
| 7 | 5 | 8 | 3 | 6 | 1 | 4 | 2 | 9 |
| 3 | 8 | 6 | 9 | 2 | 4 | 5 | 7 | 1 |
| 2 | 4 | 9 | 1 | 7 | 5 | 8 | 3 | 6 |
| 5 | 1 | 7 | 6 | 3 | 8 | 2 | 9 | 4 |
| 8 | 2 | 4 | 7 | 9 | 3 | 6 | 1 | 5 |
| 1 | 7 | 3 | 5 | 4 | 6 | 9 | 8 | 2 |
| 6 | 9 | 5 | 8 | 1 | 2 | 3 | 4 | 7 |

**4**

| 7 | 4 | 9 | 2 | 1 | 5 | 8 | 6 | 3 |
|---|---|---|---|---|---|---|---|---|
| 5 | 8 | 6 | 4 | 9 | 3 | 2 | 7 | 1 |
| 1 | 3 | 2 | 7 | 8 | 6 | 5 | 9 | 4 |
| 6 | 7 | 3 | 5 | 2 | 9 | 4 | 1 | 8 |
| 4 | 5 | 8 | 6 | 7 | 1 | 9 | 3 | 2 |
| 9 | 2 | 1 | 3 | 4 | 8 | 6 | 5 | 7 |
| 8 | 6 | 4 | 9 | 3 | 7 | 1 | 2 | 5 |
| 2 | 9 | 7 | 1 | 5 | 4 | 3 | 8 | 6 |
| 3 | 1 | 5 | 8 | 6 | 2 | 7 | 4 | 9 |

**5**

| 6 | 5 | 2 | 3 | 9 | 4 | 8 | 1 | 7 |
|---|---|---|---|---|---|---|---|---|
| 8 | 4 | 3 | 7 | 2 | 1 | 9 | 5 | 6 |
| 1 | 7 | 9 | 5 | 8 | 6 | 2 | 3 | 4 |
| 5 | 2 | 8 | 1 | 6 | 3 | 4 | 7 | 9 |
| 9 | 3 | 6 | 8 | 4 | 7 | 5 | 2 | 1 |
| 7 | 1 | 4 | 9 | 5 | 2 | 6 | 8 | 3 |
| 3 | 6 | 5 | 4 | 1 | 8 | 7 | 9 | 2 |
| 2 | 8 | 1 | 6 | 7 | 9 | 3 | 4 | 5 |
| 4 | 9 | 7 | 2 | 3 | 5 | 1 | 6 | 8 |

**6**

| 8 | 9 | 6 | 7 | 2 | 4 | 5 | 3 | 1 |
|---|---|---|---|---|---|---|---|---|
| 2 | 1 | 4 | 3 | 6 | 5 | 9 | 7 | 8 |
| 5 | 3 | 7 | 8 | 1 | 9 | 4 | 6 | 2 |
| 9 | 4 | 5 | 2 | 3 | 8 | 7 | 1 | 6 |
| 1 | 6 | 2 | 9 | 4 | 7 | 3 | 8 | 5 |
| 3 | 7 | 8 | 6 | 5 | 1 | 2 | 4 | 9 |
| 4 | 2 | 3 | 5 | 8 | 6 | 1 | 9 | 7 |
| 6 | 5 | 9 | 1 | 7 | 3 | 8 | 2 | 4 |
| 7 | 8 | 1 | 4 | 9 | 2 | 6 | 5 | 3 |

**7**

| 1 | 4 | 5 | 6 | 8 | 9 | 7 | 2 | 3 |
|---|---|---|---|---|---|---|---|---|
| 6 | 8 | 9 | 2 | 3 | 7 | 4 | 5 | 1 |
| 3 | 2 | 7 | 4 | 5 | 1 | 6 | 9 | 8 |
| 8 | 3 | 2 | 9 | 6 | 5 | 1 | 7 | 4 |
| 9 | 1 | 6 | 3 | 7 | 4 | 5 | 8 | 2 |
| 7 | 5 | 4 | 1 | 2 | 8 | 3 | 6 | 9 |
| 5 | 7 | 3 | 8 | 1 | 2 | 9 | 4 | 6 |
| 2 | 9 | 1 | 7 | 4 | 6 | 8 | 3 | 5 |
| 4 | 6 | 8 | 5 | 9 | 3 | 2 | 1 | 7 |

**8**

| 4 | 6 | 9 | 1 | 2 | 3 | 5 | 8 | 7 |
|---|---|---|---|---|---|---|---|---|
| 7 | 2 | 1 | 8 | 6 | 5 | 9 | 4 | 3 |
| 8 | 3 | 5 | 7 | 4 | 9 | 1 | 2 | 6 |
| 6 | 1 | 4 | 3 | 5 | 8 | 7 | 9 | 2 |
| 5 | 8 | 7 | 9 | 1 | 2 | 6 | 3 | 4 |
| 3 | 9 | 2 | 4 | 7 | 6 | 8 | 1 | 5 |
| 2 | 7 | 3 | 5 | 9 | 1 | 4 | 6 | 8 |
| 9 | 5 | 8 | 6 | 3 | 4 | 2 | 7 | 1 |
| 1 | 4 | 6 | 2 | 8 | 7 | 3 | 5 | 9 |

**9**

| 9 | 4 | 7 | 8 | 6 | 2 | 5 | 1 | 3 |
|---|---|---|---|---|---|---|---|---|
| 5 | 6 | 1 | 3 | 7 | 9 | 2 | 8 | 4 |
| 3 | 8 | 2 | 5 | 1 | 4 | 7 | 6 | 9 |
| 1 | 3 | 6 | 9 | 2 | 5 | 8 | 4 | 7 |
| 7 | 9 | 8 | 6 | 4 | 3 | 1 | 2 | 5 |
| 4 | 2 | 5 | 1 | 8 | 7 | 3 | 9 | 6 |
| 8 | 5 | 3 | 4 | 9 | 1 | 6 | 7 | 2 |
| 6 | 7 | 4 | 2 | 3 | 8 | 9 | 5 | 1 |
| 2 | 1 | 9 | 7 | 5 | 6 | 4 | 3 | 8 |

**10**

| 9 | 7 | 4 | 2 | 8 | 1 | 3 | 6 | 5 |
|---|---|---|---|---|---|---|---|---|
| 8 | 2 | 6 | 5 | 7 | 3 | 9 | 1 | 4 |
| 5 | 3 | 1 | 6 | 4 | 9 | 2 | 8 | 7 |
| 6 | 5 | 9 | 1 | 3 | 4 | 8 | 7 | 2 |
| 1 | 8 | 2 | 7 | 6 | 5 | 4 | 9 | 3 |
| 3 | 4 | 7 | 9 | 2 | 8 | 1 | 5 | 6 |
| 2 | 9 | 8 | 3 | 5 | 7 | 6 | 4 | 1 |
| 4 | 6 | 5 | 8 | 1 | 2 | 7 | 3 | 9 |
| 7 | 1 | 3 | 4 | 9 | 6 | 5 | 2 | 8 |

**11**

| 5 | 8 | 2 | 7 | 1 | 9 | 6 | 3 | 4 |
|---|---|---|---|---|---|---|---|---|
| 4 | 9 | 6 | 3 | 2 | 5 | 7 | 8 | 1 |
| 7 | 1 | 3 | 4 | 8 | 6 | 2 | 9 | 5 |
| 8 | 6 | 7 | 2 | 9 | 4 | 5 | 1 | 3 |
| 1 | 5 | 9 | 6 | 3 | 8 | 4 | 7 | 2 |
| 2 | 3 | 4 | 5 | 7 | 1 | 8 | 6 | 9 |
| 6 | 2 | 1 | 9 | 5 | 7 | 3 | 4 | 8 |
| 3 | 4 | 8 | 1 | 6 | 2 | 9 | 5 | 7 |
| 9 | 7 | 5 | 8 | 4 | 3 | 1 | 2 | 6 |

**12**

| 4 | 7 | 3 | 8 | 9 | 6 | 1 | 2 | 5 |
|---|---|---|---|---|---|---|---|---|
| 6 | 1 | 2 | 3 | 5 | 4 | 8 | 7 | 9 |
| 8 | 5 | 9 | 2 | 7 | 1 | 4 | 6 | 3 |
| 2 | 6 | 1 | 9 | 8 | 5 | 3 | 4 | 7 |
| 3 | 4 | 5 | 6 | 1 | 7 | 9 | 8 | 2 |
| 9 | 8 | 7 | 4 | 3 | 2 | 5 | 1 | 6 |
| 7 | 3 | 4 | 1 | 2 | 9 | 6 | 5 | 8 |
| 1 | 2 | 8 | 5 | 6 | 3 | 7 | 9 | 4 |
| 5 | 9 | 6 | 7 | 4 | 8 | 2 | 3 | 1 |

**Dr. Gareth Moore** gained his Ph.D. at Cambridge University in the field of machine intelligence. He is highly experienced in computer software research and development, and produced his own Kakuro creation software almost as soon as the first puzzle appeared in a British newspaper. He has a wide range of media interests and has written for both American and British newsstand magazines. He now runs his own video production company, Cantab Films, and works on a range of puzzle and other websites, including www.dokakuro.com and its sister site at www .dosudoku.com.